Introduction

Welcome to Partnering with AI: A Practical Guide to Human-Machine Collaboration, your roadmap to thriving in a world transformed by generative AI.

Whether you're a business leader streamlining operations, an educator personalizing learning, a student exploring new skills, or a tech enthusiast pushing creative boundaries, this book is for you.

AI isn't just a tool—it's a partner that can amplify your potential when used thoughtfully. But with its rapid evolution, ethical challenges, and risk of obsolescence, navigating AI can feel daunting.

Drawing on real-world applications and global perspectives, this book addresses these challenges head-on. Unlike other guides that overwhelm with jargon or lack depth, we offer seven accessible yet insightful chapters packed with strategies, case studies, and exercises.

You'll learn to understand AI's mechanics, collaborate effectively, apply it in workplaces and classrooms, navigate its societal impacts, and future-proof your skills. Our goal?

To empower you to harness AI as a co-creator, not a crutch, while staying grounded in human judgment and ethics. Inspired by the gaps in earlier works, we dive deeper into AI's technical and societal nuances, ensuring relevance for novices and experts alike.

From monetizing AI in side hustles to fostering inclusive education, this book equips you to make AI work for you—today and tomorrow. Let's embark on this journey to turn AI's promise into practical, impactful reality.

Chapter 1

Understanding AI's Core: From Tokens to Transformation

Artificial Intelligence, particularly generative AI, is reshaping how we work, learn, and create.

To collaborate effectively with AI, we must first understand its inner workings—not as engineers, but as informed partners. This chapter demystifies generative AI, explaining its mechanics, strengths, and limitations in a way that empowers professionals, educators, students, and tech enthusiasts to harness it thoughtfully.

By grasping how AI "thinks," you'll be better equipped to invite it into your workflows, avoid its pitfalls, and amplify your capabilities.

What Makes Generative AI Tick?

At its core, generative AI, such as large language models (LLMs) like those powering ChatGPT or image generators like DALL·E, operates by predicting patterns.

These models are trained on vast datasets—think billions of words, images, or code snippets—to recognize and replicate patterns in human language, visuals, or other data.

The key mechanism is *token prediction*: AI breaks down input (e.g., a sentence) into smaller units called tokens (words, punctuation, or parts of words) and predicts the next token based on patterns it has learned.

For example, if you prompt an AI with "The sky is," it might predict "blue" as the next word because that sequence appears frequently in its training data. This process repeats, token by token, to generate coherent text, images, or even code.

But this predictive power has a "jagged frontier"—a term describing AI's uneven capabilities. It excels at tasks within its training patterns, like summarizing text or generating creative ideas, but stumbles on others, like complex math or reasoning beyond its data's scope.

Case Study: The Poetry Misstep

A marketing manager asked an AI to write a poem for a campaign. The result was beautifully worded but contained a factual error about the product's history. Why? The AI prioritized poetic structure over accuracy, pulling from patterns in poetry rather than verifying facts. This highlights a key lesson: AI's outputs are only as reliable as the patterns it's trained on and the human oversight guiding it.

The Strengths of Generative AI

Generative AI shines in tasks requiring creativity, pattern recognition, or rapid processing. For professionals, it can draft emails, analyze data trends, or brainstorm marketing slogans in seconds.

Educators might use it to create tailored lesson plans, while students can leverage it to explore complex topics through interactive Q&A. Tech enthusiasts will appreciate its ability to generate code or visualize data, often surpassing human speed.

Consider a small business owner who used AI to analyze customer feedback. By feeding reviews into an AI tool, they quickly identified common complaints and preferences, saving hours of manual work. This strength—handling large-scale pattern recognition—makes AI a powerful collaborator across fields.

The Limitations: Biases and Hallucinations

Despite its capabilities, generative AI has significant limitations. One is *bias*, inherited from its training data. If the data contains stereotypes or skewed perspectives, the AI may reproduce them. For instance, early AI models often described engineers as male, reflecting biases in their training texts. Modern models are improving, but vigilance is crucial.

Another limitation is *hallucinations*—confident but incorrect outputs. AI might invent facts, like claiming a historical event occurred in a fictional year, because it prioritizes plausibility over truth. This is particularly risky in professional settings, where accuracy matters.

A student using AI for research might receive a fabricated citation, while a manager relying on AI for market analysis could be misled by invented statistics.

Case Study: The Fictional Expert

An educator asked an AI to recommend experts for a panel on AI ethics. The AI provided a list of names, including a supposed "Dr. Jane Ellison" with impressive credentials.

A quick search revealed no such person existed—the AI had fabricated her based on patterns of academic profiles. This underscores the need to verify AI outputs, especially in high-stakes contexts.

The Jagged Frontier in Action

The "jagged frontier" of AI's capabilities means it's neither a universal genius nor a simple tool. It can write a compelling blog post but struggle with nuanced ethical reasoning. It can generate stunning visuals but fail at precise measurements. Understanding this frontier helps you assign AI tasks it excels at while reserving complex judgment for humans.

For example, a tech enthusiast experimenting with AI-generated art found it produced breathtaking landscapes but distorted human faces.

By recognizing this limitation, they pivoted to using AI for backgrounds while hand-editing portraits, creating a hybrid workflow that maximized both AI's strengths and human creativity.

Getting Started: Experimenting with AI

To collaborate with AI, start by experimenting with its capabilities. Try simple prompts, like asking it to summarize a report or generate ideas for a project. Notice where it shines and where it falters.

For instance, professionals might test AI by drafting a client email, then refine the tone themselves. Educators could ask AI to explain a concept at different levels (e.g., for high school vs. college students) to gauge its adaptability.

Exercise: Test the Frontier

1. Choose a task relevant to your field (e.g., drafting a proposal, explaining a concept, or generating a visual).

2. Prompt an AI tool with a clear request (e.g., "Write a 100-word project summary" or "Explain neural networks in simple terms").

3. Evaluate the output: Is it accurate? Useful? Where does it fall short? Adjust your prompt or fact-check the result.

4. Reflect: How could you combine AI's output with your expertise to achieve better results?

This hands-on approach builds intuition about AI's strengths and weaknesses, preparing you to integrate it effectively into your work or studies.

Why Understanding AI Matters

Professionals, educators, students, and tech enthusiasts—understanding AI's core is the foundation of effective collaboration. Business leaders can use AI to streamline operations but must recognize its biases to avoid flawed decisions.

Educators and students can leverage AI for learning but need to verify its outputs to ensure accuracy. Tech enthusiasts can push AI's creative boundaries but should anticipate its limitations to innovate responsibly.

By grasping how AI works, from tokens to transformation, you're not just using a tool—you're partnering with a system that amplifies your potential when guided by critical thinking.

This chapter sets the stage for the practical strategies and ethical considerations we'll explore next, ensuring you're ready to navigate the evolving landscape of human-AI collaboration.

Chapter 2

The Human-AI Partnership: Principles for Collaboration

To harness generative AI as a true partner, we need a framework that guides its integration into our work, learning, and creative processes.

This chapter introduces four refined principles for human-AI collaboration, designed to empower professionals, educators, students, and tech enthusiasts to work with AI effectively while avoiding pitfalls like over-reliance or ethical missteps.

These principles—Invite AI Thoughtfully, Stay the Human in the Loop, Define AI's Role, and Adapt to AI's Evolution—offer practical, adaptable strategies to ensure AI amplifies human capabilities.

Through examples and exercises, you'll learn to apply these principles in your own context, fostering a partnership that is both productive and responsible.

Principle 1: Invite AI Thoughtfully

AI is not a one-size-fits-all solution; it's a tool to be invited into specific tasks where it excels.

Thoughtful invitation means selecting tasks that align with AI's strengths—such as pattern recognition, rapid drafting, or idea generation —while avoiding areas requiring deep judgment or emotional nuance.

For professionals, this might mean using AI to analyze market trends but not to make final hiring decisions. Educators could employ AI to generate quiz questions but rely on human insight to assess student needs.

Example: The Marketing Brainstorm

A marketing manager used AI to brainstorm campaign slogans, prompting it with "Generate 10 slogans for a sustainable clothing brand."

The AI produced creative ideas, but some were generic or off-brand.

By refining the prompt to include brand values and target audience, the manager got more relevant results, which they then curated for the final campaign.

This shows how thoughtful prompts maximize AI's utility.

Exercise: Craft a Thoughtful Prompt

1. Identify a task in your work or studies where AI could assist (e.g., drafting an email, summarizing research).

2. Write a clear, specific prompt that includes context (e.g., "Draft a 100-word email to a client about project delays, emphasizing professionalism and empathy").

3. Test the prompt with an AI tool and compare the output to a generic prompt (e.g., "Write an email").

4. Reflect: How did specificity improve the result?

Principle 2: Stay the Human in the Loop

AI is a powerful collaborator, but it's not infallible. Staying the human in the loop means actively overseeing AI's outputs, verifying accuracy, and injecting human judgment.

This principle prevents over-reliance, which can lead to errors or ethical issues. For students, this might involve fact-checking AI-generated research summaries.

Business leaders could use AI to draft reports but review them for strategic alignment.

Case Study: The Misleading Report

A financial analyst used AI to summarize market data for a client presentation. The AI included a statistic about a competitor's revenue that seemed plausible but was incorrect.

By cross-checking the data with primary sources, the analyst caught the error, reinforcing the need for human oversight. This saved the firm from a potentially embarrassing mistake.

Exercise: Verify AI Outputs

1. Use AI to generate a short output relevant to your field (e.g., a summary, analysis, or creative piece).

2. Check the output for accuracy, biases, or gaps using reliable sources or your expertise.

3. Revise the output to correct errors or enhance its quality.

4. Reflect: What did you learn about AI's reliability for this task?

Principle 3: Define AI's Role

AI can play many roles—co-writer, analyst, tutor, or brainstormer—but its role must be clearly defined to avoid confusion or misuse. Defining AI's role involves setting boundaries and expectations for its contribution.

For educators, AI might act as a tutor's assistant, generating practice problems but not grading essays. Tech enthusiasts experimenting with AI art might designate it as a concept generator, with humans handling final edits.

Example: AI as a Co-Teacher

A high school teacher used AI to create interactive history lessons, asking it to generate scenarios like "Describe a day in ancient Rome from a merchant's perspective."

The AI provided vivid narratives, which the teacher edited for accuracy and used to spark class discussions.

By defining AI as a content generator, not a curriculum designer, the teacher ensured it enhanced, not replaced, their expertise.

Exercise: Assign AI a Role

1. Choose a project or task (e.g., planning a meeting, studying for an exam).

2. Define a specific role for AI (e.g., "Generate an agenda outline" or "Create flashcards").

3. Use AI in that role and evaluate its contribution.

4. Reflect: Did the defined role keep AI focused and effective?

Principle 4: Adapt to AI's Evolution

AI is evolving rapidly, with new models and capabilities emerging regularly. Adapting to this evolution means staying curious, experimenting with new tools, and updating your workflows.

Professionals might explore AI advancements to streamline operations, while students can use cutting-edge models to deepen research.

Tech enthusiasts, in particular, thrive on testing AI's latest features, from improved language models to multimodal capabilities.

Case Study: The Upgraded Workflow

A freelance writer initially used AI to draft blog posts, relying on an early model that required heavy editing.

When a new model with better contextual understanding was released, they experimented with it, finding it produced more polished drafts. By staying open to AI's evolution, the writer saved time and improved output quality, demonstrating the value of adaptability.

Exercise: Explore AI's Evolution

1. Research a recent AI tool or update relevant to your field (e.g., via X posts, tech blogs, or AI communities).

2. Test the new tool on a familiar task and compare its performance to a previous tool.

3. Adjust your workflow to incorporate the new capability.

4. Reflect: How did adapting to the new tool enhance your collaboration?

Applying the Principles

These principles form a flexible framework for human-AI collaboration, tailored to our audience's needs.

Business leaders can use them to integrate AI into strategic planning, ensuring thoughtful prompts and human oversight.

Educators and students can apply them to enhance learning, defining AI's role in study aids or lesson planning.

Tech enthusiasts can leverage them to push AI's creative boundaries, adapting to new tools while staying critical.

Real-World Application: The Startup Success

A startup founder applied these principles to launch a product. They invited AI to analyze customer feedback (Principle 1), reviewed the insights for accuracy (Principle 2), defined AI as a data summarizer (Principle 3), and later adopted a new AI tool for predictive analytics (Principle 4).

This structured approach led to a targeted marketing strategy that boosted sales, showing how the principles drive results.

Why These Principles Matter

For professionals, educators, students, and tech enthusiasts, these principles ensure AI becomes a partner that enhances, not overshadows, human ingenuity.

They address the risk of over-reliance, make AI accessible to novices, and provide a roadmap for navigating its rapid evolution.

By applying these principles, you'll build a collaborative mindset that prepares you for the practical applications and ethical considerations in the chapters ahead, fostering a partnership that is both innovative and grounded.

Chapter 3

AI in the Workplace: Enhancing Teams, Not Replacing Them

Generative AI is transforming workplaces, offering tools to streamline tasks, spark creativity, and amplify team productivity.

For professionals, business leaders, and entrepreneurs, AI can be a powerful collaborator when integrated thoughtfully, but it's not a substitute for human expertise, judgment, or collaboration.

This chapter explores how AI can enhance teams across industries—marketing, finance, creative, and more—while addressing risks like job disruption, ethical concerns, and over-reliance.

Through industry-specific strategies, case studies, and exercises, you'll learn to deploy AI to empower your team, aligning with the book's theme of human-AI partnership for our target audience of professionals, educators, students, and tech enthusiasts.

AI's Role in the Workplace

AI excels at tasks like data analysis, content generation, and process automation, freeing teams to focus on strategy, creativity, and relationship-building.

However, its role must be defined to complement human strengths, not overshadow them. For example, AI can draft reports or analyze customer data, but humans must interpret results, make strategic decisions, and ensure ethical alignment.

This chapter provides tailored strategies for three key sectors—marketing, finance, and creative industries—while offering principles applicable across fields.

Marketing: Amplifying Campaigns with AI

In marketing, AI can analyze consumer trends, generate content, and optimize campaigns at scale. Marketers can use AI to process thousands of customer reviews, identify sentiment patterns, and tailor messaging.

However, human oversight is crucial to ensure brand authenticity and avoid tone-deaf outputs.

Case Study: The Targeted Campaign

A mid-sized retailer used AI to analyze social media feedback on X, identifying customer preferences for eco-friendly products.

The AI suggested ad copy emphasizing sustainability, but some phrases felt generic. The marketing team refined the copy, blending AI's suggestions with brand-specific messaging, resulting in a 20% increase in campaign engagement.

This shows AI's power to inform strategy when paired with human creativity.

Strategy: AI-Powered Marketing

- **Task**: Use AI to analyze customer data (e.g., reviews, social media posts) for insights on preferences or pain points.
- **Prompt Example**: "Analyze 100 customer reviews and summarize key themes, focusing on product feedback."

- **Human Role**: Validate insights, craft authentic messaging, and monitor campaign performance.

- **Risk Mitigation**: Check AI outputs for biases (e.g., overemphasizing vocal minorities) and ensure inclusivity in messaging.

Finance: Streamlining Analysis with AI

In finance, AI can process vast datasets, forecast trends, and draft reports, enabling faster decision-making.

For instance, AI can summarize market data or predict cash flow scenarios, but human judgment is essential for strategic investments or ethical considerations like client trust.

Case Study: The Risk Assessment

A financial advisor used AI to evaluate a client's portfolio, asking it to "Summarize risks for a tech-heavy investment portfolio." The AI flagged volatility in certain stocks but included an outdated regulation.

The advisor cross-checked the data, corrected the error, and presented a robust analysis to the client, reinforcing trust. This highlights the need for human verification in high-stakes fields.

Strategy: AI-Enhanced Financial Analysis

- **Task**: Leverage AI to summarize financial data or model scenarios (e.g., budget forecasts, risk assessments).

- **Prompt Example**: "Generate a 200-word summary of market trends for renewable energy stocks, citing key risks."

- **Human Role**: Verify data accuracy, interpret implications, and communicate findings to stakeholders.

- **Risk Mitigation**: Use trusted sources to fact-check AI outputs and avoid over-reliance on predictive models.

Creative Industries: Boosting Ideation with AI

In creative fields like design, writing, or media, AI can generate concepts, draft scripts, or visualize ideas, acting as a co-creator.

However, human taste, cultural context, and originality remain irreplaceable. AI's role is to spark inspiration, not dictate outcomes.

Case Study: The Film Pitch

A screenwriter used AI to brainstorm plot ideas for a sci-fi film, prompting it with "Generate five story outlines for a dystopian future."

The AI produced intriguing concepts, but one relied on clichéd tropes. The writer selected a unique idea, refined it with character depth, and pitched it successfully to a studio.

This demonstrates AI's value as an ideation tool when guided by human vision.

Strategy: AI-Driven Creativity

- **Task**: Use AI to generate creative assets (e.g., story ideas, design mockups, taglines).

- **Prompt Example**: "Create three logo concepts for a tech startup, emphasizing innovation and simplicity."

- **Human Role**: Curate and refine AI outputs, ensuring alignment with creative goals and audience expectations.

- **Risk Mitigation**: Avoid generic outputs by using specific prompts and ensure originality to prevent plagiarism risks.

Addressing Workplace Risks

While AI enhances teams, it introduces risks that require proactive management:

- **Job Disruption**: AI can automate repetitive tasks, raising concerns about job losses. Leaders should focus on re-skilling teams, using AI to handle mundane work while humans tackle strategic roles. For example, a company automated data entry with AI, freeing staff to focus on client relations, which improved satisfaction scores.

- **Ethical Concerns**: AI can perpetuate biases or produce misleading outputs. A retailer using AI for hiring found it favored male candidates due to biased training data. By auditing the AI and adjusting criteria, they ensured fairer outcomes.

- **Over-Reliance**: Teams may defer to AI without scrutiny. A manager who accepted AI's sales forecast without review missed a market shift, costing revenue. Encouraging critical evaluation prevents such errors.

Exercise: Integrate AI into Your Workflow

1. Identify a team task where AI could assist (e.g., drafting a report, analyzing feedback, generating ideas).

2. Define AI's role and craft a specific prompt (e.g., "Summarize customer feedback from 50 survey responses, highlighting top concerns").

3. Test the AI output, verify its accuracy, and refine it with your team's expertise.

4. Reflect: How did AI enhance the task? What human input was essential?

Building an AI-Ready Team Culture

To maximize AI's benefits, foster a culture that embraces experimentation, critical thinking, and ethical responsibility. Encourage teams to:

- **Experiment Freely**: Test AI on low-stakes tasks to build confidence, like using it to draft meeting agendas.

- **Share Knowledge**: Create forums for team members to share AI successes and lessons, fostering collective learning.
- **Prioritize Ethics**: Train teams to spot biases and verify outputs, ensuring AI aligns with organizational values.

Example: The AI Task Force

A tech startup formed an "AI Task Force" to explore AI's potential. The team tested AI for project management, customer support, and content creation, documenting best practices.

By sharing findings company-wide, they boosted efficiency and empowered employees to use AI confidently, proving the value of a collaborative culture.

Why AI Enhances Teams

For professionals and business leaders, AI is a tool to augment, not replace, human potential. By applying industry-specific strategies, addressing risks, and fostering a team culture of experimentation and oversight, you can integrate AI to drive innovation and efficiency.

Educators and students can draw parallels, using these principles to enhance classroom collaboration, while tech enthusiasts can adapt them to explore AI's workplace applications.

This chapter equips you to leverage AI as a team partner, setting the stage for deeper explorations of its educational and societal impacts in later chapters.

Chapter 4

AI in Education Empowering Learning and Teaching

Generative AI is revolutionizing education by offering tools to personalize learning, enhance teaching, and foster critical thinking.

For educators, students, and tech enthusiasts, AI can act as a tutor, co-creator, or research assistant, amplifying human potential when used thoughtfully.

This chapter explores how AI can empower education without replacing the human connection central to teaching and learning, addressing ethical challenges like equity and academic integrity.

Through practical strategies, case studies, and exercises, we align with the book's theme of human-AI partnership, tailoring insights for our audience of educators, students, professionals, and tech enthusiasts.

AI's Role in Education

AI excels at tasks like generating tailored content, answering questions, and analyzing learning patterns, enabling educators to focus on mentoring and students to deepen their understanding.

However, AI must complement, not supplant, human interaction. This section provides strategies for using AI in classrooms, study routines, and educational innovation, ensuring it enhances learning while upholding ethical standards.

AI as a Tutor: Personalizing Learning

AI can act as a personalized tutor, adapting to individual student needs. It can generate practice problems, explain concepts in multiple ways, or provide feedback on drafts.

Students benefit from on-demand support, while educators can use AI to scale personalized instruction.

Case Study: The Math Breakthrough

A high school student struggling with algebra used an AI tool to practice solving equations, prompting it with "Explain quadratic equations in simple terms and provide three practice problems."

The AI offered clear explanations and tailored exercises, helping the student improve their grade. The teacher reviewed the AI's outputs to ensure accuracy, illustrating how AI supports learning when guided by educators.

Strategy: AI-Powered Tutoring

- **Task**: Use AI to generate personalized study materials (e.g., explanations, quizzes, flashcards).

- **Prompt Example**: "Create a 100-word explanation of photosynthesis for a 10th-grade student, followed by five quiz questions."

- **Human Role**: Educators verify content accuracy and adapt it to curriculum goals; students use AI to supplement, not replace, classwork.

- **Risk Mitigation**: Ensure AI explanations align with educational standards and encourage students to cross-check with textbooks or teachers.

AI as a Co-Creator: Enhancing Classroom Activities

AI can generate creative content, like historical scenarios or writing prompts, to spark engagement.

Educators can use these to design interactive lessons, while students can collaborate with AI to explore ideas or refine projects.

This fosters critical thinking and creativity, key skills for the 21st century.

Case Study: The History Simulation

A middle school history teacher used AI to create a lesson, prompting it with "Write a 200-word narrative of a day in ancient Egypt from a farmer's perspective."

The AI produced a vivid story, which the teacher edited for accuracy and used as a discussion starter. Students then collaborated with AI to write their own narratives, deepening their understanding of the era. This shows AI's potential to inspire active learning.

Strategy: AI-Enhanced Activities

- **Task**: Use AI to create engaging lesson materials or student projects (e.g., scenarios, prompts, simulations).

- **Prompt Example**: "Generate three creative writing prompts for a literature class studying dystopian novels."

- **Human Role**: Educators curate and refine AI outputs; students use them as starting points for original work.

- **Risk Mitigation**: Teach students to cite AI contributions and avoid over-reliance to maintain originality.

AI as a Research Assistant: Streamlining Inquiry

AI can summarize articles, suggest research questions, or organize notes, helping students and educators explore complex topics efficiently.

However, it requires oversight to avoid inaccuracies or biases, ensuring research remains rigorous.

Case Study: The Science Project

A college student used AI to research renewable energy, asking it to "Summarize three recent articles on solar panel efficiency." The AI provided concise summaries but included a dubious claim about a breakthrough.

The student verified the claim against primary sources, refining their project with accurate data. This highlights AI's value as a research aid when paired with critical evaluation.

Strategy: AI-Supported Research

- **Task**: Use AI to summarize sources, generate questions, or organize research.

- **Prompt Example**: "Summarize two academic articles on climate change impacts in 150 words each."

- **Human Role**: Verify sources, check for biases, and synthesize findings into original work.

- **Risk Mitigation**: Teach students to use AI as a starting point and rely on peer-reviewed sources for accuracy.

Addressing Ethical Challenges

AI in education raises ethical concerns that educators and students must navigate:

- **Academic Integrity**: AI can generate essays or solve problems, tempting students to cheat.

- A university found students submitting AI-written papers, prompting a policy requiring disclosure of AI use and emphasizing original analysis.

- Educators should teach students to use AI transparently, as a tool for learning, not a shortcut.

- **Equity in Access**: Not all students have access to AI tools or reliable internet. A rural school addressed this by providing AI-enabled devices in class, ensuring all students could benefit. Institutions must advocate for equitable access to prevent a digital divide.

- **Bias and Misinformation**: AI may produce biased or incorrect content. An educator using AI to generate history lessons noticed Eurocentric biases in its narratives. By auditing outputs and diversifying prompts, they ensured balanced perspectives.

Exercise: Design an AI-Enhanced Lesson

1. Choose a subject or topic you teach or study (e.g., biology, literature).

2. Identify a task for AI (e.g., create a quiz, explain a concept, generate a discussion prompt).

3. Craft a specific prompt and test the AI output, refining it for accuracy and relevance.

4. Reflect: How can you integrate this into a lesson or study plan while ensuring ethical use?

Fostering an AI-Ready Educational Culture

To maximize AI's benefits, schools and universities should cultivate a culture of responsible experimentation:

*   **Train Educators**: Offer workshops on using AI for lesson planning or assessment, emphasizing ethical guidelines.

- **Empower Students**: Teach students to use AI critically, with lessons on prompt crafting and fact-checking.

- **Promote Transparency**: Encourage disclosure of AI use in assignments, fostering honesty and accountability.

Example: The AI Literacy Program

A community college launched an "AI Literacy" program, training faculty to use AI for personalized feedback and teaching students to leverage it for research.

The program included guidelines on ethical AI use, reducing plagiarism incidents and boosting engagement. This model shows how institutions can integrate AI thoughtfully.

Why AI Empowers Education

For educators, AI streamlines tasks and personalizes learning, allowing more time for mentoring. Students gain a versatile study partner that supports exploration and skill-building.

Professionals and tech enthusiasts can apply these principles to lifelong learning, using AI to up skill or explore new fields.

By addressing ethical challenges and fostering a culture of critical engagement, AI becomes a catalyst for educational empowerment, aligning with our theme of human-AI collaboration.

This chapter prepares you for the broader societal implications of AI explored next, equipping you to use it responsibly in learning and beyond.

Chapter 5

Navigating AI's Societal Impact:
Ethics and Beyond

Generative AI is reshaping society, influencing culture, privacy, inequality, and global dynamics.

For professionals, educators, students, and tech enthusiasts, understanding AI's broader implications is essential to using it responsibly and advocating for its ethical development.

This chapter explores AI's societal impact, addressing ethical challenges like bias, misinformation, and inequity, while offering frameworks to navigate these issues.

Through global perspectives, case studies, and exercises, we align with the book's theme of human-AI partnership, empowering our audience to engage with AI's societal role critically and constructively.

AI's Societal Footprint

AI's capabilities—generating content, analyzing data, automating tasks—extend beyond individual use, shaping societal structures.

It influences how we communicate, work, and govern, but its benefits come with risks. This section examines AI's impact on culture, privacy, and inequality, providing strategies to address challenges while maximizing positive outcomes.

Cultural Influence: Shaping Narratives and Values

AI shapes cultural narratives through media, art, and communication.

It generates news summaries, creates viral content on platforms like X, and influences public discourse. However, AI can amplify biases or spread homogenized perspectives, diluting cultural diversity.

Case Study: The Biased Art Generator

An artist used an AI image generator to create portraits for a global exhibition, prompting it with "traditional cultural figures."

The results heavily favored Western archetypes, underrepresenting non-Western cultures. By adjusting prompts to include specific cultural contexts and auditing outputs, the artist produced a more inclusive collection.

This underscores the need to counteract AI's cultural biases actively.

Strategy: Promoting Cultural Diversity

- **Task**: Use AI to create culturally sensitive content (e.g., stories, visuals, educational materials).

- **Prompt Example**: "Generate a 200-word story about a festival in rural India, emphasizing local traditions and avoiding stereotypes."

- **Human Role**: Review outputs for authenticity and diversity, incorporating feedback from relevant communities.

- **Risk Mitigation**: Diversify prompts and cross-check with cultural experts to avoid bias or appropriation.

Privacy: Balancing Utility and Protection

AI's data-driven nature raises privacy concerns. It processes personal information for recommendations, analytics, or content generation, often without transparent consent.

Professionals using AI for customer insights or educators leveraging it for student analytics must prioritize privacy to maintain trust.

Case Study: The Data Leak Scare

A university used an AI tool to analyze student performance data, aiming to tailor support programs.

The tool inadvertently shared identifiable data due to a misconfigured setting, raising privacy concerns.

By implementing stricter data protocols and anonymizing inputs, the university restored trust. This highlights the need for robust privacy safeguards.

Strategy: Safeguarding Privacy

- **Task**: Use AI for data analysis while protecting personal information.

- **Prompt Example**: "Analyze anonymized survey data on employee satisfaction and summarize trends without referencing individuals."

- **Human Role**: Ensure data is anonymized before processing and comply with regulations like GDPR or CCPA.

- **Risk Mitigation**: Regularly audit AI tools for data security and limit data inputs to what's necessary.

Inequality: Bridging the Digital Divide

AI can exacerbate inequality if access is uneven. Wealthier organizations or regions adopt AI faster, leaving under-resourced communities behind.

Students in rural areas or professionals in developing economies may lack the tools or training to compete, widening global disparities.

Case Study: The Community AI Hub

A nonprofit in a low-income region launched an AI training hub, providing free access to AI tools and workshops for local students and entrepreneurs.

Participants used AI to improve agricultural yields and market products, boosting the local economy. This shows how targeted initiatives can democratize AI access.

Strategy: Promoting Equity

- **Task**: Advocate for or implement AI access programs in underserved communities.

- **Action Example**: Partner with schools or NGOs to provide AI-enabled devices or training.

- **Human Role**: Design inclusive programs that prioritize local needs and cultural contexts.

- **Risk Mitigation**: Monitor programs for equitable impact and address barriers like connectivity or language.

Ethical Frameworks for Responsible AI Use

To navigate AI's societal impact, we need ethical frameworks that guide its use across contexts.

These frameworks, tailored for our audience, emphasize transparency, accountability, and inclusivity.

- **Transparency**: Disclose when AI is used in decision-making or content creation. For example, a journalist using AI to summarize news should note its contribution, ensuring readers understand the process.

- **Accountability**: Hold users and developers responsible for AI's outcomes. A company deploying AI for hiring must audit for bias and correct disparities, as seen in cases where AI favored certain demographics.

- **Inclusivity**: Design AI applications with diverse perspectives. Educators creating AI-driven lessons should ensure content reflects varied cultural and historical viewpoints.

Exercise: Apply an Ethical Framework

1. Choose a scenario where AI is used in your field (e.g., generating reports, teaching, creating content).

2. Apply the transparency, accountability, and inclusivity principles (e.g., disclose AI use, audit outputs, diversify prompts).

3. Evaluate the outcome: Did the framework improve the AI's societal impact?

4. Reflect: How can you integrate these principles into your regular AI use?

Global Perspectives: AI Beyond the West

AI's impact varies globally, shaped by local economies, cultures, and policies.

In Western contexts, AI often focuses on automation and innovation, but in developing regions, it addresses challenges like healthcare access or agricultural efficiency.

Understanding these differences ensures our audience engages with AI responsibly on a global scale.

Example: AI in African Healthcare

In rural Kenya, an AI tool analyzed medical data to predict disease outbreaks, enabling faster resource allocation.

However, initial models trained on Western data misdiagnosed local conditions. By incorporating regional data and collaborating with local experts, the tool improved accuracy, showing the importance of context-specific AI.

Strategy: Global AI Engagement

- **Task**: Explore AI applications in non-Western contexts relevant to your field.

- **Action Example**: Research AI's use in education or business in a developing region via X posts or global tech reports.

- **Human Role**: Adapt findings to your work, ensuring culturally relevant applications.

- **Risk Mitigation**: Avoid imposing Western frameworks; prioritize local expertise and needs.

Countering Misinformation and Bias

AI can amplify misinformation or biases, especially in public discourse. It may generate convincing but false narratives or prioritize certain viewpoints based on training data.

Professionals, educators, and students must counteract these risks to maintain trust and accuracy.

Case Study: The Misinformation Campaign

A news outlet used AI to summarize trending X posts about a political event. The AI amplified a false claim due to its prevalence in the data.

Editors caught the error by cross-checking with primary sources, reinforcing the need for human fact-checking. This case emphasizes vigilance in AI-driven content creation.

Strategy: Mitigating Misinformation

- **Task**: Use AI to analyze or generate public-facing content while ensuring accuracy.

- **Prompt Example**: "Summarize recent articles on climate policy, citing verifiable sources."

- **Human Role**: Fact-check outputs against trusted sources and disclose AI's role.

- **Risk Mitigation**: Train teams to recognize AI hallucinations and prioritize primary data.

Why AI's Societal Impact Matters

For professionals, understanding AI's societal role ensures ethical business practices that build trust.

Educators and students can use AI to foster inclusive learning while addressing global challenges. Tech enthusiasts gain tools to innovate responsibly, considering AI's cultural and equitable implications.

By navigating AI's societal impact with ethical frameworks and global awareness, our audience can champion human-AI collaboration that benefits society broadly.

This chapter sets the stage for future-proofing AI use in the next chapter, equipping you to engage with AI as a force for positive change.

Chapter 6

Future-Proofing AI Collaboration: Adapting to Rapid Change

Generative AI evolves at a breakneck pace, with new models, capabilities, and applications emerging regularly. For professionals, educators, students, and tech enthusiasts, staying ahead of this evolution is critical to maintaining effective human-AI collaboration.

This chapter equips you to adapt to AI's rapid changes by exploring future scenarios, providing strategies for continuous learning, and offering tools to integrate new advancements into your workflows.

Aligned with the book's theme of human-AI partnership, we address the risk of obsolescence, ensuring our audience can leverage AI's potential responsibly and sustainably into the future.

The Accelerating Pace of AI

AI's development is driven by breakthroughs in model architecture, training data, and computational power.

In recent years, models have progressed from basic text generation to multimodal capabilities, handling text, images, and even code with increasing sophistication. For example, tools once limited to simple chatbots now generate detailed reports, create art, or simulate complex systems.

This rapid evolution demands adaptability—professionals must update business processes, educators must rethink curricula, and students must master new tools to stay competitive.

Case Study: The Upgraded Analyst

A data analyst relied on an AI tool for market trend reports in 2023. By 2025, a new model offered real-time predictive analytics, rendering the old tool obsolete.

By experimenting with the new model and learning its advanced prompting techniques, the analyst produced more accurate forecasts, securing a promotion. This illustrates the need to embrace AI's evolution to stay relevant.

Scenarios for AI's Future

To future-proof collaboration, consider possible trajectories for AI's development. While predictions are speculative, three scenarios provide a framework for preparation:

1. **Gradual Advancement**: AI continues to improve incrementally, with better accuracy, context awareness, and domain-specific tools. Professionals might see AI tailored for finance or healthcare, while educators could access AI tutors customized for subjects like math or history.

2. **Transformative Leap**: AI achieves significant breakthroughs, approaching general intelligence (AGI) with broad problem-solving capabilities. This could revolutionize industries, requiring rapid re-skilling and new ethical guidelines.

3. **Plateau and Specialization**: AI progress slows, focusing on niche applications. Businesses might adopt specialized AI for tasks like supply chain optimization, while students use subject-specific AI assistants.

Exercise: Scenario Planning

1. Choose a scenario (gradual, transformative, or plateau) and imagine its impact on your field (e.g., business, education, tech innovation).

2. List three ways you could adapt (e.g., learn new tools, update workflows, advocate for policies).

3. Reflect: How can preparing for this scenario enhance your AI collaboration today?

Strategies for Continuous Learning

Adapting to AI's evolution requires a commitment to lifelong learning. The following strategies help our audience stay informed and agile:

Follow AI Research and Communities

Stay updated on AI advancements through accessible sources:

- **X Platform**: Follow AI researchers, developers, and enthusiasts on X for real-time updates, tool demos, and debates. Search for hashtags like #AI or #MachineLearning to discover trending discussions.

- **Blogs and Newsletters**: Subscribe to platforms like Ethan Mollick's One Useful Thing or tech-focused publications for practical insights.

- **Academic Resources**: Explore open-access papers or summaries on arXiv for deeper technical understanding, tailored for tech enthusiasts.

Example: The Informed Educator

A high school teacher followed AI education discussions on X, discovering a new tool for generating interactive science simulations. By integrating it into lessons, they enhanced student engagement, showing how community engagement keeps educators ahead.

Experiment with New Tools

Regularly test emerging AI tools to understand their capabilities and limitations. Professionals might try new analytics platforms, while students can experiment with AI study aids. Tech enthusiasts thrive on beta-testing cutting-edge models.

Case Study: The Beta Tester

A tech enthusiast joined a beta program for a multimodal AI that combined text and image generation. By testing it for a side project—creating marketing visuals—they provided feedback that improved the tool and gained early expertise, boosting their portfolio. This highlights the value of hands-on exploration.

Strategy: Tool Experimentation

- **Task**: Identify a new AI tool relevant to your field (e.g., via X posts or tech blogs).

- **Action Example**: Test it on a low-stakes task, like drafting a memo or generating study notes.

- **Human Role**: Evaluate its performance and integrate useful features into your workflow.

- **Risk Mitigation**: Start with non-sensitive tasks to avoid data privacy issues.

Build a Learning Network

Collaborate with peers to share AI knowledge. Professionals can form workplace AI groups, educators can join faculty learning circles, and students can participate in study groups or hackathons. These networks foster collective adaptation.

Example: The AI Study Group

A group of college students formed an AI study group, meeting weekly to test tools like code generators and research assistants.

They shared prompts and troubleshooted errors, improving their skills and co-authoring a paper on AI in education. This shows the power of collaborative learning.

Integrating New AI Capabilities

As AI evolves, new capabilities—like improved reasoning, multimodal outputs, or real-time data processing—require workflow updates. The following steps ensure seamless integration:

1. **Assess Relevance**: Determine if a new AI feature aligns with your goals (еобраз: predictive analytics for business, interactive tutors for education).

2. **Test Incrementally**: Pilot the feature on a small project to gauge its impact.

3. **Train and Upskill**: Learn the feature's nuances through tutorials or community resources.

4. **Monitor Ethics**: Ensure new capabilities adhere to transparency and fairness principles.

Case Study: The AI-Enhanced Startup

A startup adopted a new AI tool for customer service, capable of handling voice and text queries. They piloted it for low-priority inquiries, trained staff to oversee responses, and monitored for biases.

The tool reduced response times by 30%, proving the value of strategic integration.

Exercise: Integrate a New Feature

1. Research a recent AI advancement (e.g., a new model or feature announced on X or tech sites).

2. Test it on a relevant task (e.g., generating visuals, analyzing data).

3. Adjust your workflow to incorporate the feature, noting improvements or challenges.

4. Reflect: How did this update enhance your collaboration with AI?

Resources for Staying Ahead

To support continuous learning, leverage these resources:

- **Online Courses**: Platforms like Coursera or edX offer AI literacy courses for all levels.

- **Communities**: Join AI-focused groups on X, Reddit, or Discord for peer insights.

- **Tool Repositories**: Explore sites like Hugging Face or GitHub for open-source AI models and tutorials.

- **Industry Reports**: Read reports from Gartner or McKinsey for business-focused AI trends.

Example: The Resourceful Manager

A marketing manager subscribed to an AI newsletter and joined an X community discussing AI in advertising. They discovered a tool for real-time ad optimization, implemented it, and increased campaign ROI by 15%. This shows how diverse resources drive adaptation.

Why Future-Proofing Matters

For professionals, adapting to AI's evolution ensures competitive advantage and operational efficiency. Educators and students stay relevant by mastering tools that enhance teaching and learning.

Tech enthusiasts lead innovation by exploring AI's cutting edge. By embracing continuous learning, experimenting with new tools, and integrating advancements ethically, our audience can future-proof their AI collaboration, aligning with the book's vision of sustainable human-AI partnership.

This chapter prepares you for the final chapter, where we cultivate an AI-ready mindset to sustain this adaptability long-term.

Chapter 7

Building an AI-Ready Mindset: Curiosity and Critical Thinking

Effective human-AI collaboration hinges on more than tools and techniques—it requires a mindset rooted in curiosity, critical thinking, and adaptability.

For professionals, educators, students, and tech enthusiasts, an AI-ready mindset empowers you to explore AI's potential, question its outputs, and integrate it responsibly into your work and life.

This final chapter provides strategies to cultivate this mindset, offering exercises to test AI's limits, stories of successes and failures, and guidance to sustain engagement with AI's evolving landscape.

Aligned with the book's theme of human-AI partnership, we address the risk of over-reliance, ensuring our audience approaches AI with confidence and skepticism to drive innovation and ethical impact.

The Core of an AI-Ready Mindset

An AI-ready mindset combines curiosity—eagerness to experiment and discover—with critical thinking, the ability to evaluate AI's outputs rigorously.

Curiosity drives professionals to test AI for new business applications, educators to explore AI-driven teaching methods, and students to leverage AI for learning.

Critical thinking ensures these experiments are grounded, preventing blind trust in AI's often convincing but imperfect results.

This mindset fosters resilience, enabling our audience to navigate AI's complexities and rapid changes.

Example: The Curious Entrepreneur

A startup founder experimented with AI to optimize inventory management, testing various prompts to forecast demand.

When initial outputs were inaccurate, their critical thinking led them to refine prompts and cross-check data, resulting in a 10% cost reduction. This blend of curiosity and skepticism exemplifies the AI-ready mindset.

Strategy 1: Experiment with AI's Limits

Curiosity thrives when you push AI to its boundaries, revealing its strengths and weaknesses. By testing AI on diverse tasks—creative, analytical, or technical—you build intuition about its capabilities and learn to anticipate errors like hallucinations or biases.

Exercise: Probe AI's Limits

1. Select a task in your field (e.g., drafting a proposal, explaining a concept, generating code).

2. Craft two prompts: one simple (e.g., "Write a 100-word project summary") and one challenging (e.g., "Write a 100-word project summary that incorporates quantum computing trends").

3. Compare the outputs, noting where AI excels or fails (e.g., accuracy, depth, coherence).

4. Reflect: What did this reveal about AI's strengths and limitations for your work?

Case Study: The Code Experiment

A student tested an AI code generator, asking it to write a simple Python script and then a complex algorithm for machine learning. The simple script worked flawlessly, but the algorithm contained logical errors.

By debugging the code and learning from the failure, the student gained deeper programming insight, showing how experimenting with AI's limits fosters learning.

Strategy 2: Fact-Check and Refine Outputs

Critical thinking requires verifying AI's outputs to ensure accuracy and relevance. AI can produce plausible but incorrect information, especially in high-stakes contexts like business reports or academic research. Developing a habit of fact-checking builds confidence in using AI while mitigating risks.

Exercise: Fact-Check AI

1. Use AI to generate a short output (e.g., a market analysis, historical summary, or technical explanation).

2. Identify at least three claims in the output and verify them using trusted sources (e.g., academic papers, official reports, or primary data).

3. Revise the output to correct errors or enhance clarity.

4. Reflect: How did fact-checking improve the output's reliability?

Case Study: The Misleading Report

A marketing manager used AI to summarize competitor data for a strategy meeting. The AI cited a competitor's revenue figure that seemed off.

By checking financial reports, the manager corrected the error, ensuring the team made informed decisions. This underscores the importance of critical validation in professional settings.

Strategy 3: Learn from AI Successes and Failures

Stories of AI's triumphs and missteps inspire curiosity and sharpen critical thinking. Successes highlight AI's potential, while failures reveal its limitations, encouraging users to refine their approach.

Success Story: The AI-Enhanced Lesson

A teacher used AI to generate interactive history quizzes, tailoring questions to students' skill levels. The quizzes boosted engagement and test scores, showing AI's power to personalize education.

The teacher's curiosity in experimenting and critical review of questions ensured their quality, demonstrating the mindset in action.

Failure Story: The Overambitious Chatbot

A small business deployed an AI chatbot to handle customer inquiries, expecting it to manage complex complaints. The chatbot gave incorrect refund information, frustrating customers.

By analyzing the failure, the business redefined the chatbot's role to simple queries, with humans handling complaints, restoring customer trust. This failure taught the value of aligning AI with its capabilities.

Exercise: Analyze a Case

1. Research an AI success or failure in your field (e.g., via X posts, news articles, or case studies).

2. Identify what drove the outcome (e.g., effective prompting, lack of oversight).

3. Propose how an AI-ready mindset could enhance the success or prevent the failure.

4. Reflect: How can you apply these lessons to your AI use?

Strategy 4: Stay Engaged with AI's Evolution

An AI-ready mindset requires ongoing engagement with AI's advancements. By following developments, participating in communities, and sharing insights, you sustain curiosity and stay prepared for change.

Example: The Community Innovator

A tech enthusiast joined an X community discussing AI art tools. They shared experiments with a new model, receiving feedback that improved their prompts.

This engagement led to a collaborative project showcased at a tech conference, highlighting how community involvement fuels curiosity and innovation.

Strategy: Build Engagement

- **Task**: Join an AI-focused community (e.g., X groups, Discord servers, or local meetups).

- **Action Example**: Share an AI experiment or ask for feedback on a project.

- **Human Role**: Contribute insights and learn from others' experiences.

- **Risk Mitigation**: Verify community information to avoid misinformation.

Sustaining the Mindset

To maintain an AI-ready mindset, integrate curiosity and critical thinking into your routine

- **Set Exploration Goals**: Dedicate time weekly to test new AI tools or prompts, keeping curiosity alive.

- **Reflect Regularly**: After using AI, assess what worked, what failed, and how you improved the outcome.

- **Teach Others**: Share your AI knowledge with colleagues, students, or peers,

- reinforcing your understanding and critical perspective.

Example: The Reflective Professional

A project manager scheduled monthly "AI experiment days" to test tools for task automation. After each session, they reflected on outcomes and shared findings with their team, leading to a streamlined workflow. This practice embedded the AI-ready mindset into their work culture.

Why an AI-Ready Mindset Matters

For professionals, this mindset ensures AI enhances productivity without compromising judgment, driving career success. Educators and students leverage it to innovate in teaching and learning, staying competitive in an AI-driven world.

Tech enthusiasts use it to push AI's creative and technical boundaries, leading innovation. By fostering curiosity and critical thinking, our audience can sustain effective, ethical human-AI collaboration, fulfilling the book's vision of partnership.

This mindset equips you to navigate AI's present and future, transforming challenges into opportunities for growth and impact.

Conclusion

As we close Partnering with AI: A Practical Guide to Human-Machine Collaboration, reflect on the journey you've taken. You've explored AI's inner workings, mastered principles for collaboration, and applied them to transform workplaces and classrooms.

You've tackled AI's societal challenges—biases, privacy, inequality—with ethical frameworks and global perspectives. You've learned to future-proof your skills, adapting to AI's rapid evolution, and cultivated a mindset of curiosity and critical thinking.

Together, these tools empower you to make AI a true partner, amplifying your creativity, productivity, and impact. The AI landscape will continue to shift, but you're ready. Professionals can now leverage AI to drive profits while fostering ethical workplaces.

Educators and students can harness it to personalize learning and spark innovation. Tech enthusiasts can push AI's boundaries, creating solutions that inspire. The key? Stay human in the loop, question AI's outputs, and embrace its potential with responsibility.

This book isn't the end—it's a launchpad. Experiment with new tools, join AI communities on platforms like X, and share your insights with others. As AI reshapes our world, you're equipped to shape it back, building a future where human ingenuity and machine intelligence thrive together. Keep exploring, stay critical, and let AI be your partner in creating a brighter, more inclusive tomorrow.

Supplementary Sections
Glossary

Generative AI: AI systems that create content, such as text, images, or code, by predicting patterns based on training data (e.g., ChatGPT, DALL·E).

Large Language Model (LLM): A type of AI trained on vast text datasets to generate human-like language, used in tools like Grok or GPT.

Token Prediction: The process by which AI predicts the next unit (word, punctuation) in a sequence to generate coherent outputs.

Jagged Frontier: A term describing AI's uneven capabilities, excelling in some tasks (e.g., text generation) while struggling with others (e.g., complex reasoning).

Hallucination: When AI generates confident but incorrect or fabricated information, often due to gaps in training data.

Bias: Systematic errors in AI outputs reflecting prejudices in training data, such as gender or cultural stereotypes.

Human in the Loop: The practice of maintaining human oversight over AI processes to ensure accuracy, ethics, and relevance.

Prompt Engineering: Crafting specific, context-rich instructions to guide AI toward desired outputs.

Multimodal AI: AI capable of processing and generating multiple data types, like text, images, and audio.

AGI (Artificial General Intelligence): Hypothetical AI with human-like reasoning across diverse tasks, not yet achieved as of 2025.

References
Books and Articles:

Russell, S., & Norvig, P. (2020). Artificial Intelligence: A Modern Approach. Pearson. Foundational text on AI mechanics.

Academic Papers:

Vaswani, A., et al. (2017). "Attention is All You Need." arXiv:1706.03762. Introduces transformer models powering modern LLMs.

Bender, E. M., et al. (2021). "On the Dangers of Stochastic Parrots: Can Language Models Be Too Big?" ACM FAccT. Discusses AI biases and ethics.

Online Resources:

Hugging Face (2025). Open-source AI models and tutorials. [huggingface.co].

X Platform (2025). AI monetization threads (e.g., @Adam_DelDuca, April 2025). Real-time insights on AI trends.

arXiv.org (2025). Open-access AI research papers. [arxiv.org].

Reports:

McKinsey & Company (2024). "The Economic Potential of Generative AI." Analysis of AI's business applications.

UNESCO (2023). "AI and Education: Guidance for Policy-makers." Frameworks for ethical AI in education.